Learning from Luke

A Study Guide to the Gospel sent to a Gentile

By Michael Penny

ISBN: 9781783645404

www.obt.org.uk

Learning from Luke

* * * * *

A Study Guide to
the Gospel written by a doctor
and sent to a Gentile

* * * * *

* * * * * * * * * *

The Open Bible Trust
Fordland Mount, Upper Basildon,
Reading, RG8 8LU, UK.

Introducing Luke

Luke first appears on the scene during Paul's second missionary journey. We read:

> So, passing by Mysia, they went down to Troas. And a vision appeared to Paul in the night: a man of Macedonia was standing there, urging him and saying, "Come over to Macedonia and help us." And when Paul had seen the vision, immediately *we* sought to go on into Macedonia, concluding that God had called us to preach the gospel to them. (Acts 16:8-10)

This is the first of the "we" sections in the Acts of the Apostles relating to Luke, showing that he was present, i.e. an eye witness, to some of the events he wrote about.

From Troas he journeyed with Paul and his companions, including Silas and Timothy. They spent some together as they travelled to Philippi and Luke may have remained there, for he was in Philippi when Paul visited that city on his third missionary journey (Acts 19:5). Then Luke travelled with Paul back to Jerusalem and there he would have come across many who could give him first-hand accounts of the time when Jesus was upon earth. Not only the Twelve Disciple and John Mark, but also James and Jude, his half-brothers, and probably Mary, from whom he gleaned the information about the miraculous conception of not only Jesus but also of John the Baptist, which opens his gospel.

And from the opening words of his gospel, it seems that Luke consulted not only people, but also documents.

> Inasmuch as many have undertaken to compile a narrative of the things that have been accomplished among us, just as those who from the beginning were eyewitnesses and ministers of the word have delivered them to us, it seemed good to me also, having followed all things closely for some time past, to write an orderly account for you, most

excellent Theophilus, that you may have certainty concerning the things you have been taught. (Luke 1:1-4)

It seems "many" had written about Jesus, which should not surprise us. Sadly, however, we do not have copies of their writings as Luke did, but Marks Gospel, and possibly Matthew's, had been written by the time Luke arrived in Jerusalem and, if J A T Robinson is correct in *The Primacy of John,* so had John's Gospel[1]. And James' letter was very early, possibly the first New Testament document written[2].

So with a wealth of people to call upon and many documents, Luke set about compiling his gospel and presents us with an "orderly" account. Whether he means it is in chronological order, as some suggest, may or may not be correct. Denis Manley in *The Chronology of the Gospel of Jesus Christ* [3]suggests Matthew is the more chronological one. In that book he also produces a table of all the events Luke includes which are in neither Matthew nor Mark. It seems Luke had some extra sources.

Luke addressed his gospel to the "most excellent Theophilus", a person of some repute and with a Gentile name. This may be why Luke omitted certain unfavourable remarks about the Gentiles (e.g. compare Matthew 10:1-5 with Luke 9:1-5) and why he included some favourable quotations from the Old Testament (e.g. Luke 4:25-27).

Being a Gentile, and not being familiar with the Jewish Scriptures (our Old Testament) and Jewish culture, Theophilus would have struggled with a more Jewish gospel like Matthew. Luke seems to have been aware of this and his gospel is, in some way, more straightforward and why some today suggest it is the best gospel to give to people to introduce them to the person of Jesus Christ.

---

[1] For more on the dating of John's writing see *John: His life and writings* by Michael Penny (OBT),

[2] For more on this see *James: His life and letter* by Michael Penny (OBT).

[3] Published by The Open Bible Trust (OBT).

Introduction

Over 700 questions

Compiled by Michael Penny

These questions first appeared in a series published in *Search* magazine, and they were so well received that it has been decided to publish them so that other may benefit from them.

We suggest the reader may like to:

- First read right through the Gospel of Luke.
- Then to read the whole of the particular chapter being studied.
- Then to read the section on which a group of questions is based.

This will give the reader the context of the questions.

Try to answer the questions on that section and this can be done either in private study or in a group fellowship who can discuss the questions.

Questions on Luke Chapter 1

Luke 1:1-4 The Introduction

1. How many people had undertaken to write an account about the life of the Lord Jesus Christ?
2. From which people did Luke get the information for his account?
3. For whom did Luke write his account? (And what does his name mean?)
4. Why did Luke write his account?

Luke 1:5-25 The Birth of John the Baptist is Foretold

5. Where was Zechariah when the angel of the Lord appeared to him and what was he doing?
6. For what had Zechariah often prayed?
7. When was the future son, John, to be filled with the Holy Spirit?
8. What was to be the ministry of John?
9. Zechariah asked for a sign and was given one. What was it?
10. The people were wondering why Zechariah was so long in the temple. How did he inform them that he had seen the angel of the Lord?
11. After she became pregnant, why did Elizabeth say that the Lord "has shown me favour and taken away my disgrace among the people"? Why did she use the word disgrace?

Luke 1:26-38 The Birth of the Lord Jesus Christ is Foretold

12. Why was Mary greatly troubled by the angel's presence and words?
13. With what words did the angel reassure her?
14. Mary was not married so what was the most pertinent issue on her mind?
15. Did Mary understand the angel's explanation?

16. Did she accept it?
17. When Zechariah asked a question (v 18) he was struck dumb. When Mary asked a question (v 34) it was answered fully with no accompanying judgement. Why was Zechariah struck dumb and Mary not?

Luke 1:39-45 Mary visits Elizabeth

18. How far is it from Nazareth to the hill country of Judah?
19. What happened when Elizabeth heard Mary's voice?
20. When Elizabeth was filled with the Holy Spirit, what did she do?
21. Why did Elizabeth say Mary was blessed? (What does blessed mean?)
22. Could Elizabeth have had someone or something in mind when she uttered the words of verse 45?

Luke 1:46-56 Mary's Song

23. What does Mary say about the humble?
24. What does she say about the proud?
25. To fully comprehend Mary's song a good understanding of the Old Testament History of Israel is needed but which verses clearly indicate that she was thinking primarily of Israel?
26. How long did Mary stay with Elizabeth?

Luke 1:57-66 The Birth of John the Baptist

27. What were the people going to call the boy?
28. Why did the people object to the name John?
29. Why were the people astonished when Zechariah wrote "His name is John"?
30. What was the result of Zechariah writing "His name is John"?
31. Having suffered from God's judgement for nine months what did

Zechariah do when he could speak again?

32. What was the effect on the neighbours?

33. What did the people who heard of these events say?

Luke 1:67-80 Zachariah's Song

34. When Zechariah was filled with the Holy Spirit, what did he do?

35. Why is this song of Zechariah's called "The Benedictus"? The structure of this song is as follows:

v 68 God has visited (come)
    v 69 Horn of Salvation
        v 70 His Holy prophets
            v 71 Saved from Enemies
                v 72-73 Remember His covenant
            v 74-75 Deliverance from Enemies
        v 76 The Prophet
    v 77 Knowledge of Salvation
v 78-79 Dayspring (rising sun) has visited (come)

You may care to compare and contrast the balancing members of the structure.

36. Again to fully understand Zechariah's song a good understanding of the Old Testament is needed but which verses and words clearly indicate that he was thinking primarily of the people of Israel?

37. What was the first thought Zechariah expressed in this song?

38. How many times does Zechariah refer to redemption, salvation and the like?

39. What is the central member of the structure and what important truth does it teach?

40. What happened to the infant John?

Questions on Luke Chapter 2

Luke 2:1-7 The Birth of the Lord Jesus Christ

1. Who issued the decree that a census be taken?
2. Where did people have to go to register?
3. Why did Joseph have to go to Bethlehem?
4. How long did it take Mary and Joseph to travel from Nazareth to Bethlehem?
5. What happened to Mary when she was in Bethlehem?

Luke 2:8-20 The Shepherds and the Angels

6. What was the reaction of the shepherds at seeing the angels?
7. Did the angels tell the shepherd the precise place where the Lord Jesus was born?
8. What sign did the shepherds have to look for in their search for the baby Jesus?
9. In verse 16 the word *found* means discovered after a search. How many other places had the shepherds looked before they found the right one and how many people had they told about the angels' message?
10. What was Mary's reaction to all these events?
11. What was the shepherds' reaction?
12. What was the reaction of those to whom the shepherds spoke?

Luke 2:21-40 The Baby Jesus is presented at the Temple

13. Why was He circumcised on the eighth day?
14. When had He been given the name Jesus?
15. Why did Mary and Joseph offer a sacrifice in the temple at Jerusalem?
16. What special revelation had been given to Simeon?
17. When Simeon said "my eyes have seen your salvation" to what or to whom was he referring?

18. What did Simeon mean by what he said to Mary? (vs 34-35)

19. Who else spoke about the child Jesus and to whom did she speak?

Luke 2:41-52 The Boy Jesus at the Temple

20. Why did Mary and Joseph go to Jerusalem each year?
21. Why did it take Mary and Joseph three days to find the boy Jesus?
22. Where did they find Him and what was He doing?
23. What was everyone's reaction to His answers to their questions?
24. What was Mary's and Joseph's reaction?
25. Did Mary and Joseph understand what He said to them in verse 49?
26. What was Mary's reaction to all these events?

Questions on Luke Chapter 3

Luke 3:1-20 John the Baptist Prepares the Way

1. When did the Word of God come to John the Baptist?
2. What were the two aspects of John's baptism?
3. What does repentance mean?
4. Do Isaiah 40:3-5 and Malachi 3:1, and their contexts, help in understanding Luke 3:4-6?
5. For what two reasons was John annoyed with the crowd?
6. Which words of John's in verses 11, 13 and 14 are applicable to today?
7. Who were the people thinking John might be?
8. How did John answer these ideas?
9. When did the baptism with the Holy Spirit take place?
10. Has the baptism with fire taken place?
11. Is the baptism with fire associated with the judgement of verses 11 and 17?
12. Why did Herod eventually lock up John?

Luke 3:21-38 The Baptism and Genealogy of the Lord Jesus

13. Why was the Lord Jesus baptized?
14. What did He do after He had been baptized?
15. What happened then?
16. Why was there a voice from heaven?
(a) for the benefit of the Lord Jesus?
(b) for the benefit of John the Baptist?
(c) for the benefit of the disciples?
(d) for the benefit of the crowd?
(e) for some other reason?
17. How old was the Lord Jesus when He began to minister?
18. The genealogy in Matthew goes back only as far as Abraham whereas the one in Luke goes right back to Adam. Why this difference?

19.Compare and contrast the two genealogies of Matthew 1:1-16 and Luke 3:23-38. How many differences are there? (Appendix 99 of *The Companion Bible* will be a help.)

20.Why are there these differences?

Questions on Luke
Chapter 4

Luke 4:1-13 The Temptation of the Lord Jesus Christ

1. What is the significance of the period *forty days*?
2. The Lord Jesus answered the three temptations with three quotations.
(a) What were the three quotations?
(b) Are there any lessons we can learn from them?
(c) Where did the three quotations come from?
(d) Is there an important lesson here for us?
3. Does the Lord Jesus reject Satan's claim that the authority and splendour of all the kingdoms of the world had been given to him and that he could give them to whomever he wishes?
4. In Luke 4:10, 11, Satan quoted Psalm 91:11, 12. Why didn't he quote verse 13?
5. Make two columns on a sheet of paper. In the left hand one write out Matthew 4:1-11 and in the right hand one write out Luke 4:1-13.
(a) How many differences are there between the two passages?
(b) What was the different result, in each case, to the three temptations?
(c) Do these passages describe the same period of testing?
   Note: Appendix 116 of *The Companion Bible* will be a help here.

Luke 4:14-30 The Lord Jesus Christ at Nazareth

6. After the temptations where did the Lord go and what did He do?
7. Although the Lord taught in many other synagogues, it is recorded that He *read* the Scriptures only in the synagogue in Nazareth. Why did He not read out the Scriptures in other synagogues?
8. What are the seven aspects of the prophecy of Isaiah quoted in Luke 4:18-19?

9. What is significant about the word *anointed* (v 18) and how does it relate to one of the titles of the Lord Jesus Christ?

10. Luke 4:18-19 record that the Lord Jesus read just the first 1½ verses of Isaiah 61.

(a) What is the next part of Isaiah 61:2?

(b) To what time and event does this second part refer?

(c) Why did the Lord Jesus stop half-way through Isaiah 61:2?

11. When He had finished reading the Scriptures, what did He next say?

12. What was the reaction of those that heard Him?

13. What proverb did the Lord Jesus quote at His listeners?

14. What two Old Testament passages, relating to Gentiles being blessed, did the Lord Jesus quote to His Jewish listeners?

15. Why did He quote those two passages and that proverb?

16. Is the period of 3½ years ominous?

17. What was the reaction of those that heard the Lord Jesus utter these sayings?

18. Why did His listeners change so quickly and so extremely? (Compare verses 22 and 28-29.)

19. How did the Lord Jesus combat their attempt to kill Him?

Luke 4:31-41 The Lord Jesus Christ at Capernaum

20. Why were the people amazed at His teaching?

21. What was the testimony the demons gave concerning the Lord Jesus?

22. Why did He tell the demons to be quiet?

23. What were the three results of the Lord commanding the demon to come out of the man (One in each of verses 35, 36 & 37)?

24. Was Peter married?

25. What was the demons' testimony about the Lord Jesus?

26. Why did He not allow them to speak?

27. How did the demons know He was the Christ?
28. Why didn't the Lord Jesus want the testimony of demons?
29. Why didn't the Lord Jesus stay with the people at Capernaum?
30. What was one of the reasons why the Lord Jesus was sent?

Questions on Luke Chapter 5

Luke 5:1-11 The Lord Jesus at Gennesaret

1. What is the other name for the Lake of Gennesaret?
2. Why did the Lord Jesus teach the people from a boat?
3. When He had finished teaching, what instruction did He give Peter?
4. What was Peter's reply?
5. Was it unusual to catch fish there during the day time?
6. What did Peter say to the Lord after they had caught the fish? (Note: This is an acknowledgement of what a person *is*, not what they *have done*; see Exodus 20:19; Judges 13:22; 1 Samuel 6:20; 2 Samuel 12:13; Job 40:4 & 42:2-6; Isaiah 6:5).
7. What did the Lord next say to Simon Peter?
8. What did Peter, James and John do?

Luke 5:13-26 The Lord Jesus Heals

9. Why did the Lord Jesus instruct the man healed of leprosy not to tell anyone?
10. Why did He tell him to show himself to the priest?
11. What reaction did this miracle bring from the people?
12. Why did the Lord Jesus often withdraw to pray?
13. From where did the Pharisees and doctors of the law come to hear the Lord Jesus?
14. What was the first thing the Lord Jesus said to the paralytic man who had been lowered from the ceiling?
15. What did the Pharisees and teachers of the law think about those words?
16. Were they correct in what they thought?
17. Was the Lord Jesus claiming to be God revealed in the flesh?
18. How did healing the man demonstrate that the Lord Jesus did have the power to forgive sins?
19. Was the man healed completely or partially?

20. Was he healed slowly or instantly?

21. What effect did this healing have on:

(a) the man?

(b) the people?

Luke 5:27-39 The Calling of Levi

22. What was Levi's other name?

23. What was his profession?

24. What did the Lord Jesus say to Levi?

25. What was the complaint made by the Pharisees and teachers of the law?

26. To whom did they complain but who answered them and what was his reply?

27. Who are the righteous who do not need to repent?

28. Did the disciples of the Lord fast often?

29. Did the Law of Moses demand fasting and, if so, when and how often?

30. To what was the Lord Jesus Christ alluding in verse 35?

31. Did the disciples fast after the event alluded to?

32. Did anyone, at that time, understand to what the Lord was alluding in verse 35?

33. What does the parable of the patch mean, verse 36?

34. What does the parable of the wineskins mean, verses 37-38?

35. What does the parable of the old and new wine mean, verse 39? (Careful: remember that those to whom the Lord spoke appreciated that old wine was in *actual* fact better than new wine.)

36. Is it easy to get to the *true* meaning of a parable, as opposed to thinking of a possible application of it?

37. Do parables make Christ's teaching easier to understand? (See Matthew 13:10-17.)

Questions on Luke Chapter 6

Luke 6:1-11 The Lord and the Sabbath

1. When the disciples picked the ears of corn and ate them, did their actions break the Law of Moses or just contravene the Pharisaic additions to that Law. (See Leviticus 23:39-40)
2. Why did the Lord Jesus raise the subject of David eating the consecrated bread? (Recorded in 1 Samuel 21)
3. Was it permissible for David to eat the consecrated bread and if so, why?
4. In healing the man with the shrivelled hand on the Sabbath was the Lord Jesus breaking the Law of Moses or just the extra restrictions added by the Pharisees?
5. Why were the Pharisees furious? Why did they not see the miracles as signs which testified that the Lord Jesus was the Messiah?

Luke 6:12-26 Blessings and Woes

6. Why had the great crowd of people come? (Two reasons.)
7. Why were the people cured?
8. Are the words of the Lord Jesus in verses 20-49 addressed to all the crowd or to just His disciples?
9. Write out the structure of verses 20-26. (Hint: note the contrast between the poor and the rich, the hungry and the well fed, those who weep and those who laugh; those who are insulted and those who are spoken well of. Compare also what is said of the true prophets and the false prophets.)
10. What is the reason for people hating, excluding, rejecting and insulting the disciples?

Luke 6:27-36 Love for your Enemies

11. How were the disciples to love their enemies? (Three aspects.)
12. Verses 29 & 30 contain four commands the Lord gave to His

dsciples at that time; which, if any, are not applicable today and why not?

13.Verses 31 to 34 contain four further commands which the Lord gave to His disciples at that time; which ,if any, are not applicable today and why not?

14.Why did the Lord give such commands at that time?

Luke 6:37-42 Judging Others

15.Verse 37 records the command that the disciples were to forgive to be forgiven; is this truth for today? (See Ephesians 4:32.)

16.How great are God's rewards?

17."Can a blind man lead a blind man?" What does the Lord mean by this?

18.How much bigger than a speck is a plank? Is the Lord exaggerating or using figurative language to demonstrate a point? What point?

Luke 6:43-49 Trees and Builders

19.Why had the disciples to bring forth good things?

20.Where do the words of the mouth originate?

21.Should people who knew Jesus Christ but who did not put into practice His commands have called Him *Lord*?

22.Explain verses 48 and 49; what does the torrent represent?

Questions on Luke Chapter 7

Luke 7:1-10 The Centurion at Capernaum

1. Was the centurion a Jew or a Gentile?
2. Why did the centurion not go to see the Lord Jesus?
3. Who did he send in his place?
4. For what two reasons did they ask the Lord Jesus to help the centurion?
5. Why didn't the Lord Jesus go into the centurion's house to heal the servant?
6. How much faith did the centurion have in the Lord Jesus?

Luke 7:11-17 The Widow at Nain

7. Why did the Lord Jesus raise the widow's son from the dead?
8. What two effects did this have on the people there?
9. What two things did they say?
10. What was the effect in Judea and the surrounding country?

Luke 7:18-23 The Disciples of John

11. Why did John's disciples have to tell him these things? (See Luke 3:20.)
12. For what reason did John send his disciples to the Lord Jesus?
13. Was John doubting that Jesus was the Christ?
14. Did the Lord Jesus answer John's disciples directly?
15. What did He tell the two to say to John?
16. Would this answer John's question if he knew his Scriptures? (See Isaiah 29:18 and 35:4-6 for example.)

Luke 7:24-35 Christ's Testimony to John

17. Why did the Lord suggest that they may have gone out to see:
(a) a reed swayed by the wind?
(b) a man dressed in fine clothes?

(c) a prophet?

18. Which of the above best fits John, but what was his true role?

19. What was the Lord's testimony concerning John?

20. Why did nearly all the people agree with the Lord's testimony, but why did the Pharisees and experts of the law disagree? (Is there not a deeper reason?)

21. How did Christ describe that generation, and was it a compliment?

22. Was the life style of John and the Lord Jesus very different?

23. Whose life style did the people prefer?

24. What did Christ mean by "wisdom is proved right by all her children"?

Luke 7:36-50 The Weeping Woman

25. Why was the woman weeping?

26. To whom did the Pharisee make his comment concerning the woman?

27. Who replied to that comment, and how did he know what it was?

28. Why were the woman's sins forgiven her?

29. What was the response of the people to the Lord telling her that her sins had been forgiven?

30. What had saved this woman?

Questions on Luke Chapter 8

Luke 8:1-15 The Parable of the Sower

1.Who was with the Lord Jesus on His travels?

2.To whom did the Lord Jesus *tell* the parable?

3.Does the parable describe one sowing or four? (That is: does the farmer sow the seeds on the path one day, then sow the seeds on the rocks another day, then amongst the thorns on the third day and, some time later, sow them on the good soil?)

4.When a farmer goes out to sow, upon which type of soil would he sow most of his seeds?

5."He who has ears to hear, let him hear." What does this expression mean?

6.Was the meaning of the parable obvious to the disciples?

7. Why did the Lord Jesus explain the parable *only* to the disciples?

8.Why did the Lord Jesus speak in parables to the others? (See Matthew 13:10-17.)

9.What is represented by

(a) the seed?

(b) the path?

(c) the rock?

(d) the thorns?

(e) the good soil?

10.Has this parable received a fulfillment?

11.Would we have understood the parable without the Lord's explanation?

Luke 8:16-25 A Lamp on a Stand and the Storm on the Lake

12.Why does no one put a lamp in a jar or under a bed?

13.When will all things be disclosed and brought out into the open?

14."Whoever has will be given more; whoever does not have, even what he has will be taken from him." Do these words apply to a person's knowledge of God? Is that why the Lord Jesus said, "Therefore consider carefully how you listen."?

15. Who came to see the Lord Jesus, and why couldn't they get to Him?
16. How close to the Lord Jesus are those who hear God's Word and are obedient?
17. Why did He rebuke the disciples with "Where is your faith?"
18. How did the Lord Jesus calm the storm?
19. What effect did this have on His disciples?

Luke 8:26-39 The Healing of the Demon-possessed Man

20. How did the demon-possessed man know that the Lord Jesus was the Son of the Most High God?
21. Why was the demon called Legion?
22. Why did Legion not want to go into the Abyss?
23. Why did the Lord Jesus allow Legion to go into the pigs?
24. Were the people who saw the man healed and dressed pleased? What was their reaction?
25. What did the people of that region ask the Lord Jesus Christ to do and why?
26. Why was the man not allowed to go with the Lord Jesus, and what happened to him?

Luke 8:40-56 A Dead Girl and a Sick Woman

27. What happened when the woman touched the Lord's cloak?
28. Why did she touch the edge?
29. How did the Lord Jesus know someone had touched him?
30. What had happened to Jairus' daughter?
31. Who went with the Lord Jesus into Jairus' house?
32. How did the Lord Jesus describe death?

33. After raising the girl to life, what command did the Lord give the parents, and why?

Questions on Luke Chapter 9

Luke 9:1-9 The Lord Jesus sends out the Twelve

1. What were the twelve sent out to do?
2. What were they sent out with and why?
3. For what purpose was a bag used?
4. Why was Herod perplexed?
5. Did Herod think that the Lord Jesus was John the Baptist raised to life?
6. What did Herod want to do, and why?

Luke 9:10-17 The Feeding of the Five Thousand

7. When the twelve returned, what did they do?
8. Why did the Lord Jesus and the twelve want to withdraw themselves?
9. When the crowds followed, what was the Lord's initial reaction, and what did He do?
10. What were the disciples concerned about, and what solution did they suggest?
11. What was the Lord's solution?
12. There were twelve baskets full of broken pieces left. How many baskets would five loaves have occupied?
13. To which aspect of Christ's deity does this miracle testify?

Luke 9:18-27 Peter's Confession

14. Who did the ordinary people think the Lord Jesus was?
15. What was Peter's view?
16. Why did the Lord instruct the disciples not to tell anyone at that time?
17. What was their reaction when He told them He was to suffer, die and be raised to life? (This was the first He had said of this.)
18. What does the Lord mean by:
(a) take up his cross daily, and

(b) whoever wants to save his lifewill lose it, but whoever loses his life will save it?

19. How can a person lose or forfeit his very self?

20. Did the Lord say definitely that some of the twelve would not die before they saw the kingdom of God? (See *The Companion Bible* note of v 27 and on Matthew 10:23; 16:28; 23:39 & 24:34.)

Luke 9:28-36 The Transfiguration

21. Why did the Lord Jesus take Peter, James and John with Him?

22. What happened to the Lord Jesus when He was praying, and by what means did this happen?

23. Who also appeared, what did they talk about, and why did they describe it as a fulfillment?

24. How did Peter know who the other two men were?

25. Was Peter right to suggest building three shelters, and if not, why not?

26. Why did the three not tell anyone what they had seen?

Luke 9:37-45 The Healing of the Boy with an Evil Spirit

27. Why could the disciples not heal the boy - because of his lack of faith or theirs?

28. Did the Lord Jesus have any difficulty in healing the boy?

29. What did He next say to his disciples, and did they understand?

30. Why was this, and other things, hidden from them?

Luke 9:46-62 The Disciples and Would-be Followers

31. What were the disciples arguing about, and why?

32. How can the least be the greatest?

33. Why did John want to stop the man healing in the Lord's name?

34. Why did the Samaritans not welcome the Lord and His disciples?

35. What did James and John want to do to the Samaritans, and why? Did the Lord agree with them?

36. Why did the Lord say to the man who said he would follow, "Foxes have holes and birds of the air have nests, but the Son of Man has no place to lay his head."

37. What did the man mean by the euphemism, "Lord, first let me go and bury my father"?

38. What did the Lord mean by, "Let the dead bury the dead"?

39. Was it wrong for a person to say goodbye to his family and if so, why?

40. Why was the person who puts his hand to the plough and looks back not fit for the Kingdom of God?

Questions on Luke Chapter 10

Luke 10:1-16 The Seventy-two are Sent Out

1. Were the twelve, mentioned in Luke 9:1-6, part of the seventy-two?
2. Why did the Lord send them out in pairs?
3. Who is the Lord of the harvest?
4. For what purpose was the bag?
5. Compare the instructions given to the twelve in Luke 9:3 with those given to the seventy-two in Luke 10:4. Are the differences significant and if so, in what way are they significant?
6. Why were they not to greet anyone on the road?
7. How would their peace return to them?
8. Why were they not to move round from house to house?
9. Why did they have to ensure that all people knew that the Kingdom of God was near?
10. In what way was the Kingdom of God near?
11. Why will it be more tolerable for Tyre and Sidon than for Korazin and Bethsaida at the judgment?
12. Why is Capernaum to go down to the depths?

Luke 10:17-23 The Seventy-two Return

13. Were the seventy-two surprised that the demons obeyed them?
14. When did Satan fall like lightning from heaven?
15. To what extent did they have authority over the power of Satan, and is such extensive authority available to believers today?
16. From what did the seventy-two have protection, and is that protection available to believers today?
17. Why were they to rejoice? Because of the authority and the protection that they had or for some other reason?
18. To whom is the Lord referring when he speaks of:
(a) wise and learned?
(b) little children?

19.How can people know the Father?

20.In what way were the disciples especially blessed?

Luke 10:24-37 The Good Samaritan

21.For what reason did the expert ask the Lord Jesus about eternal life?

22.What was the expert's reply to the Lord's questions about the law?

23.Did the expert give the correct answer, and is that answer valid for today?

24.Why did the expert want to know who was his neighbour?

25.Leaving aside the parable, in real life who was most likely to help the Jew, and who was the least likely?

26.What happened in the parable? Who did not help the Jew, and who did?

27.What point did the Lord Jesus want to get over to the expert?

Luke 10:38-42 Mary and Martha

28.What was Mary doing?

29.What was Martha doing?

30.Why did Martha complain?

31.Were Mary's actions right:

(a) for that time?

(b) for all time?

32.Was Martha wrong to be concerned about hospitality? If not, why not, and what was her mistake?

Questions on Luke Chapter 11

Luke 11:1-13 Teaching on Prayer

1. How long was the prayer the Lord Jesus taught His disciples?
2. Where is God's King to come?
3. The word translated "daily" is *epiousios*, which means, literally, coming upon or descending upon. Has "give us each day descending bread" any Jewish significance either in their past or in their future, or both?
4. For what reason did the man rise and give his friend three loaves?
5. Are the promises of verses 9 and 10 for all believers at all times? If not, to whom were they given, and for when?
6. Similarly, the statement of verse 13; did people in the Acts period, or do people in this age, have to ask for the Holy Spirit? If not, to whom do these words refer, and for when?

Luke 11:14-28 Beelzebub

7. Who is Beelzebub?
8. Were their sons able to cast out demons?
9. What is the meaning of verses 21-2? Can anyone be associated with the strong man or the stronger man?
10. What is the meaning of verses 24-26? Is the man literally a man, or is it a figure for the nation of Israel?
11. Who are blessed? What does blessed mean?

Luke 11:29-36 The Sign of Jonah and the Lamp of the Body

12. Why were they a wicked generation?
13. What was the sign of the prophet Jonah?
14. Why will the Queen of the South condemn that generation at the judgment?
15. Why will the men of Nineveh condemn that generation at the

judgment?

16. Is the Lord referring to literal eyesight in verse 34? If not, to what is he referring?

17. How can the light within be darkness (v 35)?

Luke 11:37-54 Six Woes

18. Why was the Pharisee surprised?

19. Did the Pharisee say anything to the Lord?

20. To whom are the six woes addressed?

21. What did the Pharisees not do, and what should they have done?

22. What did the Pharisees love?

23. To what are the Pharisees likened? Were they important?

24. What did the experts of the law do to the ordinary people?

25. Why did the experts build tombs for the prophets if they approved of their forefathers killing them?

26. Why was that generation to be held responsible for the blood of all the prophets from Abel to Zechariah?

27. What did the experts take away?

28. *Who* did they hinder going *where*?

29. Why did the Pharisees and the teachers of the law oppose the Lord fiercely.

Questions on Luke Chapter 12

Luke 12:1-12 Warnings and Encouragements

1. What is the yeast of the Pharisees, and why is it likened to yeast?
2. The expression "I tell you" is used to introduce an important subject, in this case **fear**. Why were they **not** to fear men?
3. Who were they to fear and why?
4. Where will Christ acknowledge those who have acknowledged Him?
5. What constitutes blasphemy against the Holy Spirit? (See Matthew 10:20-32.)
6. Why should they not fear when brought before synagogues, rulers and authorities? Is this truth for today?

Luke 12:13-21 The Parable of the Rich Fool

7. What were they told to be on their guard against, and has this any relevance to today's materialistic society?
8. What did the rich man do and say? Did it seem sensible to him, and would it seem sensible to many in an atheistic pleasure seeking industrialized world?
9. What happened to the rich man? Does this happen to all?
10. Was he wrong to store up things for himself, or was something else missing as well?

Luke 12:22-34 Do Not Worry

11. What did the Lord tell the disciples not to worry about?
12. Why were the disciples told not to worry about all these things?
13. Did these instructions and reasons apply to Christians in the Acts period? Do they apply to Christians today?
14. What were the disciples told to seek?
15. What were they told to sell, and are these instructions applicable to today? If not, when were they relevant, and why?

Luke 12:35-48 Watchfulness

16. Who is the master, and what does the wedding banquet symbolize?
17. Has the master on any occasion dressed himself to serve his servants?
18. Why were they to be ready?
19. What will be the reward of the manager who cares for the servants under him?
20. The servant who mistreats the men and women servants will be "cut in pieces" and "assigned a place with unbelievers". Is this literal or symbolic?
21. Some servants will be beaten with many blows and others with few blows. Is this literal or symbolic? If symbolic, what does it symbolize?

Luke 12:49-59 Peace and Division

22. What fire is it that the Lord wished had already been kindled?
23. What baptism had the Lord still to undergo?
24. The object of the Lord's coming was peace, but the effect was division. Will He ever bring peace to this earth and if so, when?
25. Should the people have been able to interpret the times? If so, from where could they have got the information, and is there a lesson here for Christians today?
26. Who should have judged on behalf of the people what was right? Who should judge for you today?
27. If people let others judge for them, what might be the consequences?

Questions on Luke Chapter 13

Luke 13:1-9 Accidents and Evil

1. Were the Galileans that Pilate killed greater sinners than other Galileans?
2. Were the people who died in the accident at the tower of Siloam greater sinners than the rest of the Jerusalem population?
3. Are people who are killed in accidents and by other means today greater sinners than those who live to an old age and die of natural causes? If not, why do they suffer and die before they reach three-score years and ten?
4. Christ told those people that if they did not repent, they would suffer. Did they repent and, if they didn't, how and when did they suffer?
5. Who or what is represented by the fig-tree and vineyard? (See Judges 9:7-15 and Isaiah 5:1-7.)
6. Have the three years and one more year any significance? If so, what?
7. Did the fig-tree bear fruit? If not, when was it cut down?

Luke 13:10-21 Healings and Parables

8. How long after the Lord laid His hands on the woman did she recover completely?
9. Why was the synagogue ruler upset, and did he have any grounds for his reaction?
10. Why was the Lord Jesus Christ's action correct?
11. In prophetic and allegorical passages of Scripture are birds generally symbols of evil or good?
12. What does the mustard tree represent? (Compare Deuteronomy 7:7 and Genesis 12:2.)
13. Is there an occasion in the New Testament where yeast is clearly used to represent good?
14. What is the result of the woman's action - a slow improvement or a slow corruption?

15. What is improved or corrupted?

Luke 13:22-30 The Narrow Door

16. Is this parable about certain specific people? If so, which ones?
17. Who does the owner of the house symbolize?
18. The owner of the house refuses access to those who are evil doers. As *all have sinned and come short of the glory of God*, what specific evils have these people done?
19. Who are those who will come from the north, east, south and west?
20. Are the *first* the Jews in the land of Palestine and the *last* the twelve tribes scattered abroad; i.e., the dispersed of Israel? If not, who are the *first* and *last*?

Luke 13:31-35 Sorrow Over Jerusalem

21. Why did the Pharisees, traditionally the enemies of the Lord Jesus, warn Him about Herod?
22. How long before the death and resurrection of Christ did this event take place?
23. What is the goal that Christ is to achieve on this third day?
24. Why did Christ say, "no prophet can die outside of Jerusalem"?
25. Why did He not gather to Himself the people of Jerusalem?
26. Did the inhabitants of Jerusalem see the Lord Jesus after His resurrection and say to Him, "Blessed is He Who comes in the name of the Lord"? If they didn't, when will they do this?

Questions on Luke Chapter 14

Luke 14:1-6 Healing Dropsy

1. Why was the Lord Jesus being carefully watched?
2. What are the visible symptoms of dropsy?
3. According to the Law of Moses, was it lawful to heal on the Sabbath or not?
4. What visible changes would be seen in the man to indicate clearly that he had been healed?
5. How did the Lord Jesus make it clear to the people that healing on the Sabbath was obviously lawful?
6. What was their answer?

Luke 14:7-14 Places of Honour

7. How are places at a wedding reception arranged today? How were they arranged in Israel at the time of the Lord Jesus?
8. Where are the places of honour situated at a wedding reception today? Where were they situated in Israel at the time of the Lord Jesus?
9. Why shouldn't a person take a place of honour unless specifically invited? What might happen; where could he end up; and how would he feel?
10. Where should a person sit? What might happen, and how would he feel then?
11. What was the Lord Jesus trying to teach the guests of this prominent Pharisee with this illustration? Is there a lesson in this for twentieth century Christians?
12. Why should the Pharisee not invite his friends and neighbours, his brothers and relatives to a meal? Should Christians today not invite their friends and neighbours, their brothers and families for a meal?
13. Who should the Pharisee invite and why? Was this command, and associated promise, for that time and situation?

Luke 14:15-23 The Parable of the Great Banquet

14.One at the table said, "Blessed is the man who will eat at the feast in the kingdom of God". What did he mean by this? Was he agreeing with what he had just heard?

15.Notice that **when** the man **was preparing** the great banquet, he sent out invitations. Then later, **when the banquet was ready,** he sent a reminder to those who **had been invited,** so had any of the people valid excuses for not attending the banquet?

16.Would a person buy a field without first looking at it?

17.Would a person buy five yolk of oxen without first trying them out?

18.Why should being newly married prevent a person attending a banquet?

19.When the servant reported the excuses, what was the master's reaction and new orders?

20.What were his further orders on being told there was still room - who could fill the empty places, and who could not?

21.Is this a parable about the nation of Israel? If so:

(a) When was the original invitation sent out, and who delivered it?

(b) Who was sent to tell the people everything was ready?

(c) Which people in Israel made the excuses?

(d) Which people are symbolically described as the poor, the crippled, the blind and the lame?

(e) Who are those out in the roads and country lanes?

(f) What, exactly, does the banquet represent?

Luke 14:24-34 The Cost of Being a Disciple

22.Does the Lord Jesus mean that His followers must *literally* hate their families? If not, what does He mean? (Compare John 15:12.)

23.What does Christ mean by His followers having to "carry a cross"?

24. What do people say of a man who fails to complete a building he has started? What will people say of those who follow the Lord Jesus for a time and then give up?

25. Christ tells the crowds that those who want to be His disciples must give up *everything*. Did any do that, and is this command applicable today?

26. If someone started to be a disciple and then gave up, to what did Christ liken him?

27. Why did the Lord say, "He that has ears to hear, let him hear?" What does this expression mean? (See Appendix 142 of *The Companion Bible*.)

Questions on Luke Chapter 15

Luke 15:1-7 The Parable of the Lost Sheep

1. To whom was this parable addressed?
2. Would a shepherd **normally** leave in the open country, unprotected, ninety-nine sheep and go and search for one?
3. Would he **normally** continue to search and search for that one until he found it?
4. Would the losing and finding of a sheep be a relatively common occurrence? If so, would a shepherd **normally** call all his friends and neighbours to celebrate the finding of one lost sheep?
5. In view of Christ's words seemingly running against the **normal** course of events, is there a touch of irony in what He is saying? If so, at whom or what is it aimed? If not, why has He painted such an **abnormal** picture?
6. Who is represented by the shepherd, and who by the sheep - if anyone?
7. Who are the **"you"** so pointedly addressed in verse 7?
8. Were there ninety-nine righteous people in Palestine in Christ's day? Are there ninety-nine in the world today? Are there any?

Luke 15:8-10 The Parable of the Lost Coin

9. To whom is this parable addressed?
10. Often in parables, prophecies or allegorical writing in the Bible, the figure of a woman symbolizes something bad or someone evil. Is this the case in this parable?
11. Who does the woman symbolize - if anyone?
12. A silver coin is worth a day's wages, so if a woman had ten such coins and then lost one, would she carefully search and search until it was found?
13. Would the losing and finding of a day's wages be a relatively

common experience? When it happened, would a person call friends and relatives for a celebration?

14.Who are the **"you"** so pointedly addressed in verse 10?

15.Would these people appreciate the point made in verse 7 and repeated in verse 10? Do we appreciate it?

Luke 15:11-32 The Parable of the Lost Son

16.To whom is this parable addressed?

17.Who is represented by the older son; who by the younger; and who by the father?

18.To what share of the property was the younger entitled?

19.Did the younger son get his share and, if so, what did he do with it?

20.Did the older son get his share of the property and, if so, what did he do with it?

21.Many gospel messages have been preached on this parable, but are these verses dealing with the repentance of an unsaved sinner, or with the turning of one who knew God and had backslidden? (Note that the father-son relationship is there from the beginning of the parable.)

22.What was the attitude of the older son when the younger returned?

23.Is this attitude similar to that of the Pharisees and teachers towards the tax gatherers and sinners?

24.Do the closing words of this parable emphasize the teaching of verses 7 and 10?

25.What are these three parables trying to teach the Pharisees and teachers? Are there any lessons for us here? If so, what are they?

Questions on Luke Chapter 16

Luke 16:1-13 The Parable of the Shrewd Manager

1. To whom are these verses addressed?
2. Is this a parable or is it direct teaching?
3. Why could the manager not continue with his duties?
4. What was the manager's reaction to being accused of wasting the rich man's possessions?
5. What were the manager's actions following this accusation?
6. Why did the rich man commend the manager?
7. "For the people of this world are more shrewd in dealing with their own kind than are the people of light."

(a) Are these words part of the parable; i.e., part of the words of the rich man?

(b) Are the words *not* a part of the parable, but are direct teaching from the Lord?

(c) Who were the children of the light?

(d) In what ways were the children of the light not shrewd when dealing with one another?

(e) Are these words true of Christians today? If so, in what ways are they not shrewd when dealing with one another?

8. *"I tell you*, use worldly wealth to gain friends for yourself, so that when it is gone, you will be welcomed into eternal dwellings."

(a) Are these words part of the parable; i.e., said by the rich man? If so, what does he mean by *"eternal dwellings"*?

(b) Are these words *not* part of the parable, but are direct teaching from the Lord? If so:

　(i) What does the Lord mean by *"eternal dwellings"*?

　(ii) Is the Lord really telling people to "use worldly wealth to gain friends for yourself, etc."?

　(iii) If these words are a direct statement by the Lord Jesus Christ, *The Companion Bible* suggests that the opening words should be translated, "and, do I say unto you...?" -

i.e., a rhetorical question demanding the answer "No!" to what follows, with verses 10-12 giving the reasons why He does *not* teach people to use wealth incorrectly. Is this interpretation possible and likely?

9. What are the *true* riches to which Christ refers?

10. What would the disciples understand by the *property of your own* mentioned by Christ?

Luke 16:14-18 The Pharisees and the Law

11. What expression does Luke use to describe the Pharisees?

12. What was their reaction to the Lord's teaching of the shrewd manager?

13. What did they try to do in the eyes of men?

14. What, in the context of this passage, does man highly value but God detest?

15. How were people *forcing* themselves into the Kingdom of God?

16. Did the Lord Jesus Christ uphold the Law in His ministry?

17. For what reason did the Pharisees allow divorce?

18. Did the Law permit divorce and, if so, for what reasons? (Deuteronomy 24:1-4)

19. Bearing in mind the Lord's words in verse 17, and in Matthew 5:17-18, what *exactly* is He teaching in verse 18? (Compare Matthew 5:31-32)

20. Is there a break in the narrative between verses 18 and 19?

Luke 16:19-31 The Rich Man and Lazarus

21. To whom are the words of verses 19-31 addressed?

22. The *parable* of the Lost Son commences with the words, "There was a man." The *parable* of the Shrewd Manager opens with "There was a rich man." This section opens with "There was a rich man." Does this indicate this passage is a parable?

23.If this is *not* a parable, but is *direct truth*:

(a) Why is the rich man in torment and agony?

(b) Genesis 13:2 states that Abraham was *very* wealthy: why was he not being tormented?

(c) Why was Lazarus in comfort?

(d) What wrongs had the rich man done to deserve torment?

(e) What good things had Lazarus done to deserve eternal comfort?

(f) Does the passage tell us that the rich man had rejected God?

(g) Does the passage tell us that Lazarus had believed and worshipped God?

(h) Would Lazarus actually be in comfort if he could observe and hear people in torment?

(i) Where else in the Scripture is the word *torment* used to describe the state of people after death?

(j) If the rich man is in torment simply because in this life he had good things, what is the eternal fate of *all* living in the affluent industrialized world of today?

24.If this is *not* direct truth but is parable:

(a) Who, in the parable, would the Pharisees associate with themselves?

(b) For them, who would Lazarus represent?

(c) Most parables are based on well known events or teachings of the time. Was this idea of the poor being rewarded after death and the rich suffering part of the popular teaching of that day? If so, who taught it?

(d) Did the Pharisees believe all that Moses and the Prophets taught?

25.How many times does the expression *Abraham's side (Abraham's bosom, KJV)* occur in the Scriptures?

26.What did the Pharisees understand by *Abraham's side* (bosom), and was their idea based on Scripture or on the teaching their ancestors brought back from Babylon? (See *The Works of Josephus: Discourse to the Greeks concerning Hades.*)

27. Were they convinced when one rose from the dead? If not, why not?
28. Is the one being referred to here the Lord Jesus Himself or Lazarus of Bethany?

Questions on Luke Chapter 17

Luke 17:1-10 Sin, Faith and Duty

1. Do these verses follow on from the teaching of the previous chapter?
2. What sort of *things* which cause people to sin did the Lord have in mind? What sort of *things* in our society cause people to sin?
3. Who are the *little ones* that the Lord mentions?
4. What does the word *rebuke* mean?
5. How many times a day had they to forgive? How many times in a lifetime?
6. Was it necessary for a brother to repent for him to be forgiven?
7. Does the Lord Jesus tell the disciples how to increase their faith?
8. Is verse 8 literal or allegorical? If the latter, what does the verse teach?
9. What does a master ask of his servants?
10. If the disciples are described as *unprofitable* servants, what description is appropriate for ourselves?

Luke 17:11-19 Ten Healed of Leprosy

11. Why did the men with leprosy stand at a distance?
12. Why did the Lord Jesus tell the lepers to show themselves to the priests?
13. How many of the healed lepers came back to thank the Lord?
14. Why was the man called a foreigner? Were the others not foreigners?
15. Why did the Lord heal the foreigner?
16. Verse 19 states that "Your faith has made you well".
(a) If this is the case, what was the reason for the other nine being healed?
(b) The word translated *made well* is more often translated *save*. Would it make more sense in this context to say to the one leper who praised God, "Your faith has *saved* you"?

Luke 17:20-37 The Coming of the Kingdom of God

17. Who asked when the Kingdom of God would come?

18. The Lord states that "the kingdom of God is *within* you", but the footnote has *"among* you". As these words are addressed to the arch enemies of Christ, it seems inappropriate to say that "the kingdom of God is within you". Thus, the translation *"among* you" seems more likely to be correct. How was the kingdom of God *among* them?

19. Why will the disciples long to see one of the days of the Son of Man, days like those they were then seeing?

20. Why should the disciples not bother to listen to those who say that the Son of Man is here or there?

21. Lightning lights up the sky from one end to the other, and everyone can see it and knows it. Will it be like this on the day of the Son of Man? That is, will everyone be aware of this day?

(a) Everyone in Palestine?

(b) Everyone in the world?

22. What must happen before the day of the Son of Man?

23. Before this special day, however, the situation will be as it was in the days preceding:

(a) the flood? What were the conditions like then?

(b) the destruction of Sodom? What were conditions like then?

24. The conditions of the days of Noah and the days of Lot will occur again before the day of the Son of Man. Will these conditions exist:

(a) throughout Palestine?

(b) throughout the world?

25. Why should those on the rooftops not get their goods from inside their houses?

26. Why should those in the fields not go back to the house for anything?

27.What happened to Lot's wife? How is her situation an example here?

28.Are the words of verse 33 peculiar to the days just prior to the day of the Son of Man? If so, what do they mean?

29.Are the persons *taken*, in verses 34-36, taken in judgement, or are those *left* for judgement?

30.What did the disciples mean by the question, "Where Lord?", and does He answer the question?

31.What do the Lord's words in verse 37 mean? Where will the dead bodies and the vultures be? When does this occur?

Questions on Luke Chapter 18

Luke 18:1-8 Prayer and Persistency

1. How should the disciples pray?
2. Were they to pray always about the same thing?
3. Why did the unjust judge give in to the widow's request?
4. Is God like the judge?
5. The unjust judge delayed answering the widow for selfish reasons. Why did God delay bringing about justice?
6. Who are the *chosen ones* referred to in verse 7?
7. Has God brought about justice for His *chosen ones* yet? If not, when will He do so?
8. When the Son of Man comes, will He find faith on the earth? (Luke 17:26-30.)

Luke 18:9-17 Righteousness and Humility

9. Why did the Lord Jesus tell this parable and to whom does it apply today?
10. Did the Law prescribe fasting twice a week? (Leviticus 16:29; Numbers 29:7)
11. Did the Law prescribe giving a tenth of everything? (Deuteronomy 14:22-23)
12. Why did the tax collector beat his chest and not look up to heaven?
13. Why did the tax collector consider himself a sinner?
14. In the Greek, the tax collector says, "God, have mercy on me, *the* sinner". Has this any significance?
15. Why was the tax collector justified and the Pharisee not?
16. Why did the disciples rebuke people for bringing babies to the Lord Jesus?
17. What characteristics of a little child had the Lord Jesus in His mind when He said, "For the kingdom of God belongs to such as these (children)"?
18. "Receive the kingdom of God like a little child." What does this

mean?

Luke 18:18-30 Eternal Life and Treasure

19. Why is no one but God good?
20. What must the ruler do to inherit eternal life, and how does this compare with John 3:16?
21. Why was the ruler sad when he was told to sell everything?
22. If the ruler sold everything, would he secure for himself eternal life, or something more?
23. In this passage, is the Lord Jesus dealing with the gift of eternal life, or with treasure in heaven and reward?
24. What does to "enter the Kingdom of God" mean? Is this dealing with salvation or a place with the overcomers in the millennial kingdom on earth?
25. Did the disciples receive much in this life?
26. Is it true today that *all* who forsake much for the kingdom of God receive many times as much in this lifetime? If not, will they ever receive anything for what they have forsaken?

Luke 18:31-43 Death and Healing

27. Why did the Lord Jesus take the disciples aside to tell them of His death?
28. Why did the disciples not understand what He had told them?
29. How was the meaning of what He said hidden from them?
30. Why did those who led the way for the Lord Jesus rebuke the blind man for shouting?
31. What did the blind man want?
32. The NIV has, "Your faith has *healed* you," but the *KJV* has "Your faith hath *saved* thee." Which is the better translation and why? (See question 16 on Luke 17.)
33. Did the blind man follow the Lord Jesus, and was he saved?

Questions on Luke Chapter 19

Luke 19:1-10 Zacchaeus

1. What does the name Zacchaeus mean?
2. Was he one of the ordinary tax collectors?
3. Why did he want to see the Lord Jesus Christ?
4. Why did the Lord want to stay at Zacchaeus' house?
5. For what reasons did the people consider Zacchaeus a sinner?
6. What caused Zacchaeus to want to give half his possessions to the poor?
7. Why pay back *four times* the amount to anyone he had cheated?
8. What was Christ's comment on this change in Zacchaeus?

Luke 19:11-27 The Parable of the Ten Minas

9. For what reason did the Lord Jesus tell the people this parable?
10. Herod the Great and his son, Archelaus, had recently left Jericho, where they had built a palace, for Rome to receive the sovereignty - Josephus, *Antiquities of the Jews* 17:13:1. Thus, Christ continues to base his parables upon well known events and circumstances. In this one, who or what are represented by:
(a) the man of noble birth?
(b) the distant country?
(c) the ten servants?
(d) the ten minas?
(e) his subjects?
11. Why did the man's subjects not want him to be their king?
12. Why give ten cities to the man who had earned ten minas, but only five to the man who had earned five?
13. Was the man who made none wicked? If so, why? Was he a liar and a hypocrite?
14. Why was that man's mina taken from him and given to the man who had ten?
15. Verses 26 & 27 are the Lord's own application of the parable.

What do they mean?

16.Does verse 26 refer to a person's relationship with the Lord? (Compare Luke 8:16-18 and note question 14 on Luke 8.)

17.Were those who refused to have the man rule over them killed? If so, when?

Luke 19:28-40 The Triumphant Entry

18.How did the Lord know that in Bethany there would be tied a colt upon which no one had ridden?

19.Why did the owners of the colt allow the disciples to take the animal?

20.Why did the disciples put the Lord Jesus on the colt?

21.Why did the people spread their cloaks on the road for the colt to walk on?

22.For what reasons did the crowd praise God?

23.Why did the Pharisees ask Christ to rebuke His disciples when they were singing Psalm 118:26, and why didn't He do so?

Luke 19:41-48 Jerusalem and the Temple

24.For what reason did Christ cry when He saw Jerusalem?

25.What could have brought peace to the city, and why couldn't they now see it?

26.When did the days spoken of in verse 43 come to Jerusalem?

27.Are verses 43 & 44 describing in more detail that spoken of in verses 26 & 27?

28.Why was Jerusalem and its inhabitants to suffer such calamity? Did they do so and, if so, when?

29.For what reasons did Christ drive out of the temple those who were selling?

30.Why could the Jewish leadership find no way of killing Christ?

Questions on Luke Chapter 20

Luke 20:1-8 Christ's Authority is Questioned

1. What two questions did the chief priests, teachers and elders ask the Lord Jesus?
2. What was His question in reply?
3. Why would they not answer His question?
4. Why didn't He give a direct answer to their original questions?
5. Was it obvious from where His authority came?

Luke 20:9-19 The Parable of the Tenants

6. In the parable of the tenants, who or what is represented by:
(a) the man?
(b) the vineyard?
(c) the farmers?
(d) the servants?
(e) the son?
(f) the others to whom the vineyard was to be given? (Note: the word for *others* means *others of the same kind*.)
7. What does this parable mean?
8. Is it prophetic? If so, has the vineyard been given to the *others*? If so, when; if not, when will it be?
9. "May this never be!" is the opposite of "Amen!" Why did the people say this?
10. What is the meaning of:
(a) the stone the builders rejected has become the capstone?
(b) Everyone who falls on the stone will be broken to pieces?
(c) He on whom the stone falls will be crushed?
11. Why did the teachers and priests want to arrest the Lord, and why didn't they?

Luke 20:20-26 Taxes

12. Why did the teachers and priests send people to spy on Christ?

13. The spies told Christ that what He said and taught was right and that He did not show partiality but taught the way of God in accordance with truth. Why did they say all this?
14. What was a denarius, and how much was it worth?
15. Was it right to pay taxes? Is it ever right to withhold taxes?

Luke 20:27-40 Marriage and Resurrection

16. What was one of the Sadducees' peculiar teachings?
17. Why did they ask about the woman married to the seven brothers? What was their point?
18. How do people of this age differ from those considered worthy to have part in the resurrection from the dead? (Three aspects.)
19. Are resurrected people like angels in all respects, or just some? If some which ones?
20. How can a person be "considered *worthy* of taking part in the resurrection from the dead"?
21. How does Moses at the burning bush show that the dead are to be raised?
22. Had Abraham, Isaac and Jacob been raised from the dead at:
(a) the time of Moses?
(b) the time of Christ?
If neither, when will they be?
23. In verse 38, the *NIV* has "for to him all are alive." *The Companion Bible* suggests it should read "for all (in resurrection) live by him". Which is the better?
24. Why did some of the teachers who earlier opposed Christ support Him with, "Well said teacher!"?

Luke 20:41-47 David's Son?

25. Is Christ the son of David, a descendant of David?
26. If so, how could David call Him Lord, implying His existence at

David's time?

27. What were the six failures of the teachers of the law?

28. Do any of these failures have an application to any today?

29. In what ways were the teachers of the law severely punished?

Questions on Luke Chapter 21

Luke 21:1-4 The Widow's Gift

1. The temple treasury was situated in the woman's court, occupying about 200 square feet and surrounded by a colonnade. Inside, against the wall, were thirteen receptacles - nine for legal dues and four for voluntary contributions. Were the rich people and the widow paying their legal dues or making voluntary contributions?
2. What were the legal dues?
3. In Mark 12:43, the Lord Jesus states that "this poor widow has put more into the treasury than *all* the others." What did he mean by this?

Luke 21:5-10 Signs Preceding the Destruction of the Temple

4. Did the Lord Jesus answer specifically the disciples' questions on time, "*When* will these things happen?" If not, why not?
5. What is the first thing He warns them about?
6. What two claims will some make who will tempt the disciples to follow them, and is there an application of this to people of other ages - even for us today?
7. Wars and revolutions have happened throughout the history of the world, so how can these be a sign?
8. Similarly, nations and kingdoms rising against one another, earthquakes, famines and pestilences have occurred many, many times. How can these be significant signs?
9. As these words were spoken to the disciples in Jerusalem, and as verses 21 and 24 mention Judea and Jerusalem, then is it possible that the wars and revolutions, the rising of nations and kingdoms, the earthquakes, famines and pestilences refer to events which were or are to take place in the vicinity of Jerusalem and Judea and the surrounding countries? Does this make verses 8-10 more significant? (Note: the

expression *kingdom against kingdom* is used in Isaiah 19:2 to refer to civil war in Egypt.)

10. Is there any record of such wars and revolutions, the rising of nations and kingdoms and the earthquakes, famines and pestilences occurring during the lifetime of the disciples? (See, for example, The Acts of the Apostles.)

Luke 21:12-19 Before All These Things

11. In verse 12, the Lord speaks of an earlier time than the destruction of the temple. How much earlier?
12. Has the Acts of the Apostles any record of any of the disciples:
(a) being delivered up to synagogues and prisons and being brought before kings and governors?
(b) exercising words and wisdom such that none of their adversaries was able to resist and contradict them?
(c) being betrayed by parents, brothers, relatives and friends?
(d) being put to death?
(e) being hated for following Jesus as the Christ?
13. What did Christ mean by "not a hair on your head will perish," bearing in mind that He had just told them that some would be put to death?
14. How would they *save* themselves by standing fast? Does *save* here refer to:
(a) safety in this life?
(b) initial salvation?
(c) reward as in Matthew 16:24-28?

Luke 21:20-24 Jerusalem Surrounded

15. In verse 20, the Lord spoke of the time *when* Jerusalem would be surrounded. Is this part of the *before all this* of verse 12, or does verse 20 continue on after verse 11?
16. What is the desolation spoken of in verse 20?

17. How will they know that desolation is near?

18. What are those in Judea to do, and why?

19. Why will it be so dreadful for pregnant women and feeding mothers?

20. Why will there be distress, and where will it be - throughout the world, or just in Judea?

21. Why will wrath fall, and upon whom - all nations, or just Israel?

22. What will be the result of this distress and wrath? (Josephus' *Wars of the Jews* 5:10 and 6:9.)

23. How long will Jerusalem be trampled by the Gentiles? Has that time been completed? Will it return - Revelation 11:2?

Luke 21:25-28 Signs in Heaven

24. Verse 11 speaks of *great signs from heaven* and verse 25 has *signs in the sun, moon and stars*. Does verse 25 follow on from verse 11, implying that the events of verses 12-24 precede those of verses 8-11 and 25-28? Or are just verses 12-19 dealing with earlier events?

25. What are the *great signs from heaven* of verse 11 and the *signs in the sun, moon and stars* of verse 25?

26. Are the *fearful* events of verse 11 the roaring and tossing sea of verse 25? What sea would the disciples understand by this?

27. Why will men faint with terror?

28. The climax of this whole passage is the Son of Man coming in a cloud. What else does He come with?

29. Did He have either of these at His first coming?

30. Why were they told to lift up their heads?

Luke 21:29-33 The Parable of the Fig Tree

31. What is the parable of the fig tree, and what is its meaning?

32. What is meant here by the kingdom of God?

33. Which events described in verses 8-28:

(a) came to pass in the lifetime of the disciples?

(b) are still future?

(c) could have a second fulfillment, as some prophecies do?

34. Clearly, the words of verse 32, "this generation will certainly not pass away until all these things have happened" cannot be correct! There are three explanations:

(a) The *NIV* footnote has *race* for generation.

(b) Others have suggested the verse should read *"that generation"*, referring to some future generation of Jews living in Jerusalem.

(c) *The Companion Bible* states that the word *until (eos an)* is conditional, and that Christ was teaching that all these things *could* have happened within the lifetime of that generation if ... the *if* being the Jews' acceptance of Jesus as their Messiah either before or after the cross.

Discuss these three explanations, bearing in mind Christ's strong affirmation in verse 33.

Luke 21:34-38 Words of Warning

35. Why were they to be careful, and what would weigh them down?

36. What is *that day* mentioned in verse 34?

37. Verse 35 implies that this will affect "all those who live upon the face of the *whole earth*," but verses 20-24 have clearly been dealing with Jerusalem and Judea. The word translated *earth* is *ge*, but it can be translated *land*, as it is in verse 23. Would it be possible to translate *ge* as *land* in verse 35, making it refer to Judea?

38. What two things were they to pray for?

39. Did they escape all that was to happen? If so, how?

40. Will all the disciples be able to stand before the Son of Man? Is there a lesson here for all believers of all times, and for us?

Questions on Luke Chapter 22

Luke 22:1-6 Judas and Satan

1. Why was the Feast of Unleavened Bread called the Passover? (Leviticus 23:4-8)
2. Why were the chief priests and the teachers afraid of the people?
3. Has Satan ever entered anyone other than Judas?
4. Why did Satan enter Judas?
5. As Satan entered Judas, was Judas responsible for his actions? (See verse 22.)

Luke 22:7-23 The Last Supper

6. Why did the Passover Lamb have to be sacrificed on the day of Unleavened Bread, and which day was this?
7. Why did the Lord tell Peter and John to look for a man carrying a jar of water?
8. How did He know that, when the two entered the city, they would meet a man carrying a jar of water who would have a large upper room, ready furnished for guests?
9. Has the Lord Jesus eaten the Passover with the apostles again? If so, when? If not, will He do so, and how will this "find fulfillment in the kingdom of God"?
10. Has the Lord Jesus drunk of the fruit of the vine since that evening? If so, when? If not, when will He do so; i.e., when will the kingdom of God come?
11. Who are the parties in the New Covenant? (Jeremiah 31:31-34; Hebrews 8:10-12.)
12. What are the benefits of the New Covenant for the people involved?
13. How is the New Covenant better for those people than the Old Covenant?

Luke 22:24-30 After the Supper

14. What were the disciples disputing, and was this a common discussion of theirs?
15. Who were the disciples not to be like? Who were they to emulate?
16. How should the greatest behave, and how should the person with authority act?
17. What kingdom did Christ confer on His disciples?
18. What position will the twelve have in Christ's kingdom?

Luke 22:31-34 Simon, Satan and a Change in Orders

19. When did Satan ask to sift Simon? (Cf. Job 1 & 2.)
20. What did Christ pray for Simon?
21. What instruction did He give Simon?
22. When had the Lord sent them out with no purse, no bag and no sandals, and why had He done so?
23. Why, now, was He telling them to take a purse and a bag and even a sword?

Luke 22:39-46 On the Mount of Olives

24. What did the Lord Jesus tell the apostles to pray for, and why?
25. Why did an angel from heaven need to come and strengthen Christ? (Cf. Matthew 4:11.) Was He, there in the garden, on the point of death? (Cf. Mark 14:34 & Hebrews 5:7.)
26. Which cup did Christ want removed; the one symbolizing death on the cross, or representing death in the garden? (Cf. John 18:11.)
27. Why did Judas use a kiss to betray the Lord Jesus?
28. Peter followed the arrested Christ at a distance; what happened to the rest of the apostles?

29. What three things happened just after Peter denied knowing Christ for the third time, and what was Peter's reaction to these?

Luke 22:63-71 Before the Council

30. Why did the men guarding Jesus beat Him?
31. What questions did the chief priests and teachers of the law ask Him?
32. Why were they so interested; was it out of a genuine interest, or was there some other motive?
33. Why did the Lord Jesus answer with an allusion to Psalm 110:1?
34. What did the chief priests and teachers understand by this reference?
35. Did the Lord Jesus clearly state that He was the Christ (i.e., the Messiah) and the Son of God?
36. What was the reaction of the chief priests and teachers to these words of the Lord, and why did they react in that way?

Questions on Luke Chapter 23

Luke 23:1-25 Before Pilate and Herod

1. What were the three accusations that the assembly brought against the Lord Jesus Christ?
2. Which one of these was true?
3. Was Pilate concerned enough about this one to detain the Lord?
4. Why did Pilate send the Lord Jesus to Herod?
5. Why was Herod greatly pleased to see Jesus?
6. How many questions did Herod ask the Lord?
7. Why didn't the Lord answer any of them? Did He even speak to Herod? If not, why not?
8. What exactly was it that caused Herod and Pilate to become friends?
9. What did Pilate and Herod agree to do with the Lord Jesus?
10. What was the reaction of the chief priests, the rulers and the people to that decision?
11. If they wanted Him crucified for subversion (v 2) and stirring up the people (v 5), why did they want Barabbas released when he had committed insurrection and murder (v 18)?
12. What is the difference between subverting and stirring up the people (vs 2 & 5) and insurrection (v 18)? Could Pilate see that the Jewish leaders were being inconsistent, even hypocritical?
13. How many times did Pilate state that he could find no basis for their charges against Christ?
14. How many times did he try to release Him?
15. Why did Pilate give in to their request to crucify Christ?
16. Origen (AD 186-253) has Barabbas' first name as Jesus. Could this be correct, and the Jewish people chose the wrong Jesus (Joshua) to save them?

Luke 23:16-43 The Crucifixion

17. Why was Simon from Cyrene made to carry Christ's cross?

18. When did the women of Jerusalem fulfill Christ's words and say, "Blessed are the barren women, and the womb that never bore and the breasts that never nursed", and what caused them to say it?

19. When did they say to the mountains, "Fall on us" and to the hills, "Cover us"? What caused them to utter these words?

20. Did this prophecy affect all women in Judea, or just those in Jerusalem?

21. At what time was the tree green? When was it dry? What did the Lord mean by this figure?

22. For whom was Christ praying when He said, "Father forgive them for they know not what they are doing"? (See Acts 3:12-25, and note vs 14-17; see also Acts 5:30 and 10:39.)

23. Why didn't they know what they were doing? Why did they do it in ignorance (Acts 3:17)?

24. Could Christ have saved Himself and, if He had done so, what would have been the consequences:

(a) for Him?

(b) for His people?

(c) for us?

25. What did the criminal who hurled insults from the Lord want from Him?

26. What did the other one ask for - was it life then and there, or eternal life - and did he get it?

27. The *NIV* has, "I tell you the truth, today you will be with me in paradise", but as Christ spent the next three days and nights in the tomb, this cannot be correct. As there is no punctuation in the Greek, *The Companion Bible* suggests this should read, "I tell you the truth today, you will be with me in paradise;" i.e., sometime in the future. Is the expression, "I tell you the truth today", an Hebraism - a figure of speech - similar to the one in Deuteronomy 4:26?

28. Is Paradise on earth? (See Revelation 2:7 & 22:1-2.)

Luke 23:44-56 The Death and Burial

29. The sixth hour is noon, and the ninth 3:00 p.m. As there was no eclipse of the sun, what caused the darkness?
30. Why was there darkness?
31. How was the curtain of the temple torn in two, and why?
32. What caused the centurion to praise God and say, "Surely this was a righteous man"?
33. Why did all those who had gathered to witness the crucifixion beat their breasts before they went away? Was this a sign of victory?
34. What did those who had followed the Lord Jesus do?
35. Had all the Jewish council wanted Christ crucified?
36. Why did Joseph of Arimathea want the Lord's body?
37. Why did the women prepare spices and perfumes?

Questions on Luke Chapter 24

Luke 24:1-12 The Resurrection

1. When did the women go to the tomb, and what did they find?
2. Who was in the tomb, and why did the women react in the way they did?
3. What were the women told, and should they have known this?
4. When had the Lord told them, "The Son of Man must be delivered into the hands of sinful men, be crucified and on the third day be raised up again"?
5. Which women witnessed these events, and who did they tell?
6. Why were they not believed? Weren't the apostles expecting the resurrection?
7. When he heard what the women said, what six things did Peter do?
8. Where did Peter go; what did he find, and what was his reaction?

Luke 24:13-35 The Road to Emmaus

9. What were the two on the road to Emmaus talking about?
10. How were they kept from recognizing the Lord Jesus?
11. What was their testimony concerning Jesus of Nazareth? Who did they say He *was*, and who had they *hoped* Him to be?
12. Did they, at this time, believe the women's report that Jesus was alive again?
13. Why did the Lord describe them as "foolish" and "slow of heart"?
14. The Jews of that time believed that the prophecies concerning the Messiah's *glory* would be fulfilled, but not those concerning His *sufferings*. Had the apostles made the same mistake?
15. Does the Old Testament state that the Messiah was to suffer first before He could enter His glory? If so, where? (See also v 46 & Acts 3:17-18.)
16. When the Lord explained to them what the Scriptures said

concerning the Messiah, did they know it was Him?

17. When did they recognize Him? Why did they recognize Him?

18. What happened to the Lord when they did recognize Him?

19. Why did their hearts burn when He had opened the Scriptures to them?

20. Considering that it must have been evening and dark, wasn't it brave of the two to return to Jerusalem? How long would the journey have taken them?

21. When had the Lord appeared to Simon?

Luke 24:36-49 The Lord Jesus appears to the Disciples

22. When the Lord appeared to them, what was their reaction?

23. How did the Lord try to assure them that it really was Himself?

24. Why did they still not believe - or did they?

25. What else did Christ do to show them that He was not a ghost, but had a literal, bodily resurrection?

26. How much written in the Old Testament concerning Christ must be fulfilled? How much *has been* fulfilled? What is left *to be* fulfilled?

27. What did He do to their minds?

28. What were they to preach, and where were they to preach it?

29. Why was this to be preached *first* in Jerusalem?

30. What was He going to send them?

31. Why were they to stay in Jerusalem?

Luke 24:50-53 The Ascension

32. When they were at Bethany, why did the Lord bless them?

33. What happened to Him when He was blessing them?

34. Did the disciples carry out the command of verse 49?

35. Why did they stay in the temple?

> **Having completed this study of Luke's Gospel, it would be a good idea to read right through Luke's Gospel again. This will be of great help and the reader will be surprised how much is recalled and how much has been learnt.**

Also, having gone through Luke's Gospel, you may care to consider his second piece of writing, The Acts of the Apostles, and you may care to use the following study guide.

Search The Acts of the Apostles
A Study Guide to
the Fifth Book of the New Testament

By Michael Penny and Neville Stephens

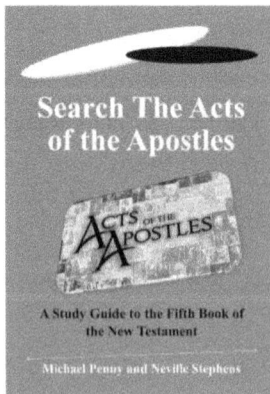

Other Study Guides

A Study Guide to Psalm 119
By Michael Penny

A very useful guide to Psalm 119 indicating …

- It is the longest Psalm;
- It is an Acrostic Psalm – and gives an acrostic translation of the first 24 verses;
- The Ten Hebrews words which recur throughout the Psalm.

Each group of eight verses is considered separately – giving 22 studies.

Each group is given in two translation presented in parallel for ease of comparison.

For each group a task is set for personals study or group discussion.

And at the end of each group, as a conclusion, there is page or so of commentary.

Manual on the Gospel of John
By Michael Penny

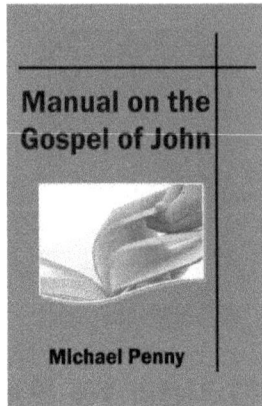

This book was produced with college students for college students, but is valuable for any age range. It asks and answers the questions the students asked about John's Gospel, but in a novel way.

The book is in four parts:

1) Aims of the Book; How to use the Book
2) Questions with Aids and Hints to the Answers
3) Questions with Answers and Further Information
4) Main themes of John's Gospel

This book is ideal for not only for personal study, but also for Youth Groups, House Groups, and Bible Study Groups. The questions in Section Two can be discussed and answered, and there and Aids and Hints to help. After being discussed and answered, the author's answers and comments can be reviewed from Section Three.

"If you are stuck for an idea with your group, try The Manual on the Gospel of John." (Eric Thorn, reviewed in *The Connexion)*

Further details of all the books on these pages
can be seen on

www.obt.org.uk

The books are available from that website and from

The Open Bible Trust
Fordland Mount, Upper Basildon,
Reading, RG8 8LU, UK.

They are also available as eBooks from Amazon and
Apple and as
KDP paperback from Amazon

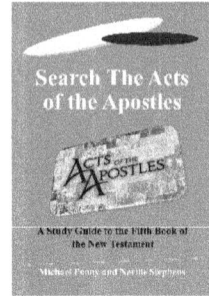

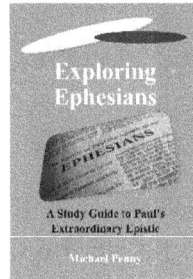

Learning from Luke
A Study Guide to the Gospel sent to a Gentile

Moving through Mark
A Study Guide to the Second Gospel

Search the Acts of the Apostles
A Study Guide to the
Fifth Book of the New Testament

Going through Galatians
A Study Guide to Paul's First Letter

Exploring Ephesians
A Study Guide to Paul's Extraordinary Epistle

About the author

Michael Penny was born in Wales in 1943. He read Mathematics at the University of Reading, before teaching for twelve years and becoming the Director of Mathematics and Business Studies at Queen Mary's College in Hampshire. In 1978 he entered Christian publishing, and in 1984 became the administrator of The Open Bible Trust.

He held this position for seven years, before moving to the USA and becoming pastor of Grace Church in New Berlin, Wisconsin. He returned to Britain in 1999, and is at present the Administrator and Editor of The Open Bible Trust. From 2010 he has been Chairman of Churches Together in Reading, where he speaks in a number of churches of different denominations. He is also a member of the Advisory Committee to Reading University Christian Union and a chaplain at Reading College.

He is lead chaplain for Activate Learning and has set up chaplaincy teams in a number of their colleges including Reading College, The City of Oxford College, Bracknell and Wokingham College, and Blackbird Leys College.

He lives near Reading with his wife and has appeared on Premier Radio and BBC Radio Berkshire many times. He has made several speaking tours of America, Canada, Australia, New Zealand and the Netherlands, as well as others to South Africa and the Philippines. Some of his many writings have been translated into German and Russian.

Also by Michael Penny

He has written many books including:

40 Problem Passages,
Galatians: Interpretation and Application,
Joel's Prophecy: Past and Future,
Approaching the Bible,
The Miracles of the Apostles,
The Manual on the Gospel of John
The Bible! Myth or Message?

Plus two written with W M Henry:

The Will of God: Past and Present
Following Philippians
Abraham and his seed (with chapters by Sylvia Penny also)

His latest three books are:

James: His life and letter
Peter: His life and letters.
Paul: A Missionary of Genius

Further details of all these books can be seen on

www.obt.org.uk

from where they can also be ordered.

They are also available as eBooks from Amazon and Apple and as
KDP paperbacks from Amazon.

Approaching the Bible
By Michael Penny

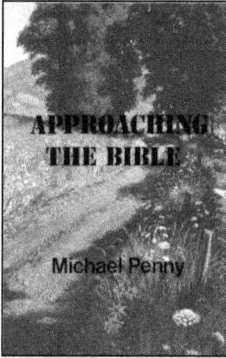

To gain a better understanding of any book of the Bible, including the Gospel of Luke, it is important to set it in the context of the other books. This is just what Michael Penny does in *Approaching the Bible*. Each book of the Bible is seen in relation to each other to gain an overall, and greater, appreciation of what the Scriptures teach about the plan and purposes of almighty God.

Reviews:
What other have said about *Approaching the Bible*!

Frank Wren, *Trumpet Sounds*
A good book for those who want to study seriously the Word of God. It delves into basic areas to lay a good foundation for understanding the message using certain guidelines set by Miles Coverdale.

Paul C. Clark, pastor, Great Kills Bible Chapel, Staten Island, NY; *Librarian's World*, official publication of Evangelical Church Library Association.
This is a thoroughgoing exposition and defense of the dispensationalist approach to interpreting the Bible. The author traces what he believes to be such an approach from some of the earliest Church Fathers onwards, points out the strengths and weaknesses in the dispensational system of modern interpreters, and advocates what he holds to be an improved approach. He sees Acts 28:28 as the watershed between God's dealings with Jews and Gentiles.

About this Book

Learning from Luke
A Study Guide to the Gospel sent to a Gentile

This book takes people through the Luke's Gospel with a series of guided questions. In all there are over 700 questions: that is about 30 questions on each chapter. These questions first appeared in a series published in *Search* magazine, and they were so well received that it has been decided to publish them so that other may benefit from them.

Individual readers can ponder these questions, meditate upon them, and consider an answer. These question can also stimulate groups to deliberate upon them and discuss them, and so come to a joint response with respect to the answers.

This is an ideal study guide to the Gospel of Luke as these questions bring out a wealth of information and teaching.

****

Publications of The Open Bible Trust must be in accordance with its evangelical, fundamental and dispensational basis. However, beyond this minimum, writers are free to express whatever beliefs they may have as their own understanding, provided that the aim in so doing is to further the object of The Open Bible Trust. A copy of the doctrinal basis is available on **www.obt.org.uk** or from:

THE OPEN BIBLE TRUST
Fordland Mount, Upper Basildon,
Reading, RG8 8LU, UK

www.ingramcontent.com/pod-product-compliance
Lightning Source LLC
Chambersburg PA
CBHW070519030426

42337CB00016B/2028